Sing a Song of Sixpence!

Sing a Song of Sixpence!

The Best Song Book Ever

Compiled by Jane Hart
Pictures by Anita Lobel

LYNX
LONDON
1988

The compiler is grateful to the following for granting permission to include copyrighted material in this collection: Page 11, "All the Pretty Little Horses," collected, adapted, and arranged by John A. Lomax & Alan Lomax TRO, copyright © 1934 and renewed © 1962 by Ludlow Music, Inc., New York, New York, used by permission. Page 77, "Five Little Chickadees," from *The Song Play Book* by Crampton and Wallaston, copyright © 1917 by A.S. Barnes Company. Page 83, "Bluebird," *Sally Go Round the Sun* by Edith Fowke, Copyright © 1969 by McClelland and Stewart Ltd. and reprinted by permission of Doubleday & Company, Inc. Page 84, "The Gallant Ship," from *The Song Play Book* by Crampton and Wallaston, copyright © 1917 by A.S. Barnes Company. Page 86, "Clap Your Hands," from *American Folk Songs for Children* by Ruth Crawford Seeger, copyright © 1948 by Ruth Crawford Seeger, reprinted by permission of Doubleday & Company, Inc. Page 93, "Gogo," by Margaret Marks and Mary Okari, from *Making Music Your Own, Book 2*, copyright © 1971 by General Learning Corporation and reprinted by permission of Silver Burdett Company. Page 97, "Three White Gulls," from Botsford Collection of Folksongs, copyright © 1933 by G. Schirmer, Inc., used by permission. Page 98, "See the Pony Galloping Galloping," composer/arranger, Roberta McLaughlin, Lucille Wood, Jacques Rupp, copyright © 1969 by Bowmar Publishing Corp. and assigned 1981 to Belwin-Mills Pub. Corp., used with permission and all rights reserved. Page 106, "Here Stands a Redbird," from *Sally Go Round the Sun* by Edith Fowke, copyright © 1969 by McClelland and Stewart Ltd. and reprinted by permission of Doubleday & Company, Inc. Page 121, "Roll Over," from *Sally Go Round the Sun* by Edith Fowke, copyright © 1969 by McClelland and Stewart Ltd. and reprinted by permission of Doubleday & Company, Inc. Page 124, "Eletelephony," from *Tirra Lirra* by Laura E. Richards, copyright © 1930, 1932 by Laura E. Richards and used by permission of Little, Brown and Company. Page 130, "The Bus Song," adapted with new music, lyrics, and arrangement, from *Eye Winker, Tom Tinker, Chin Chopper* by Tom Glazer, copyright © 1973 by Songs Music, Inc., Scarborough, New York, used by permission. Page 136, "El Coquito" (The Little Tree Toad), from *Sing a Song with Charity Bailey*, copyright © 1955 by Plymouth Music Co., Inc., New York, New York, used by permission. Page 137, "Mexican Counting Song," from *Children's Songs of Mexico*, copyright © 1963 and used by permission of Highland Music Company. Page 144, "Hanukkah Song," from *Gateway to Jewish Song*, copyright © 1939 by Behrman's Jewish Book House, Inc., and renewed © 1967 by Ginn & Company.

First published in the United States of America by Lothrop, Lee & Shepard Books, a division of William Morrow & Company Inc., in 1982 under the title *Singing Bee!*

First published in Great Britain in 1983
by Victor Gollancz Ltd
This Lynx edition published in 1988
by Victor Gollancz Ltd
All rights reserved

Printed in Italy by New Interlitho, Milan

For Daniel, Elizabeth, and Laura

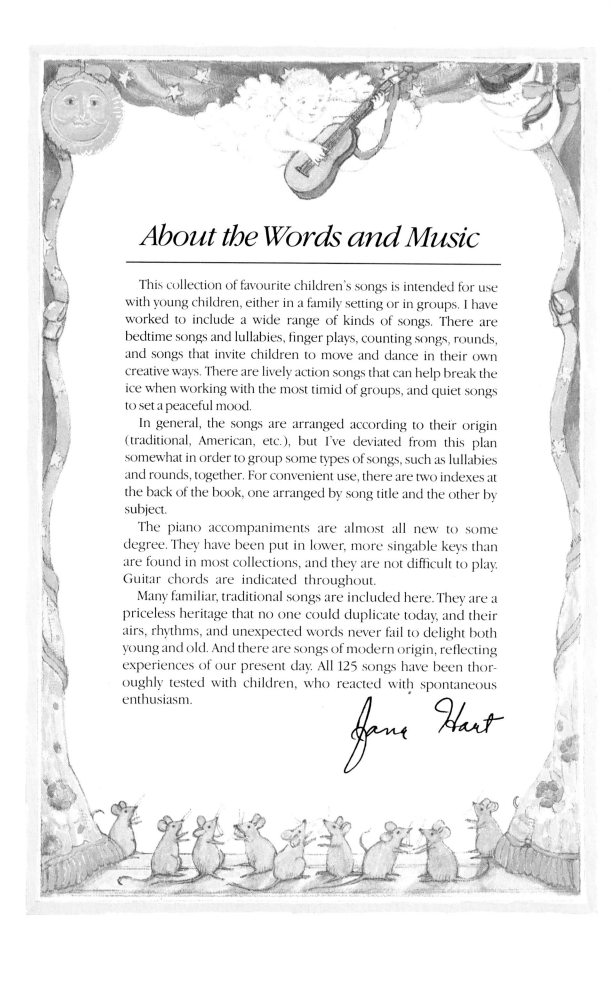

About the Words and Music

This collection of favourite children's songs is intended for use with young children, either in a family setting or in groups. I have worked to include a wide range of kinds of songs. There are bedtime songs and lullabies, finger plays, counting songs, rounds, and songs that invite children to move and dance in their own creative ways. There are lively action songs that can help break the ice when working with the most timid of groups, and quiet songs to set a peaceful mood.

In general, the songs are arranged according to their origin (traditional, American, etc.), but I've deviated from this plan somewhat in order to group some types of songs, such as lullabies and rounds, together. For convenient use, there are two indexes at the back of the book, one arranged by song title and the other by subject.

The piano accompaniments are almost all new to some degree. They have been put in lower, more singable keys than are found in most collections, and they are not difficult to play. Guitar chords are indicated throughout.

Many familiar, traditional songs are included here. They are a priceless heritage that no one could duplicate today, and their airs, rhythms, and unexpected words never fail to delight both young and old. And there are songs of modern origin, reflecting experiences of our present day. All 125 songs have been thoroughly tested with children, who reacted with spontaneous enthusiasm.

Jane Hart

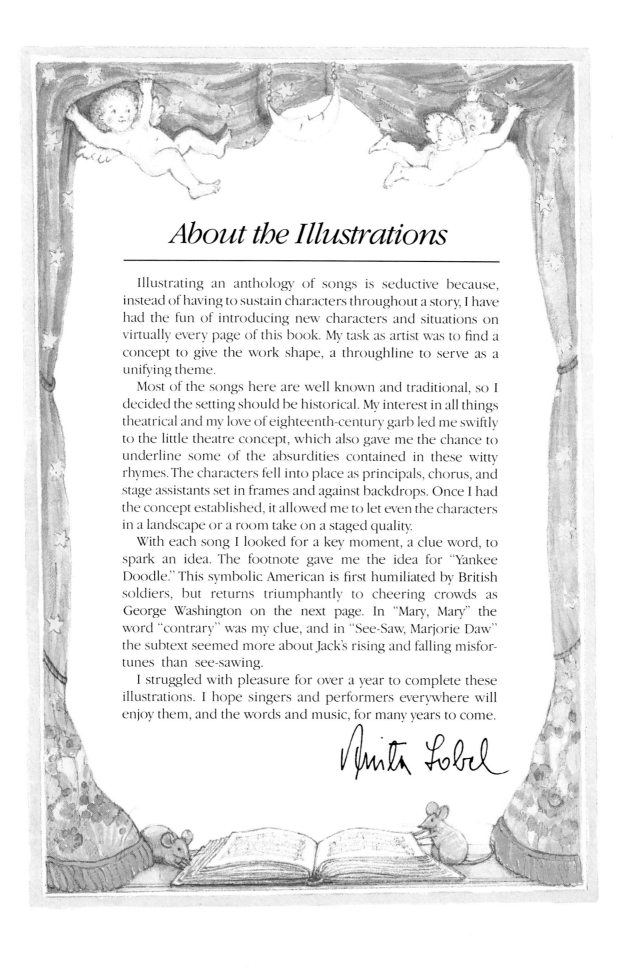

About the Illustrations

Illustrating an anthology of songs is seductive because, instead of having to sustain characters throughout a story, I have had the fun of introducing new characters and situations on virtually every page of this book. My task as artist was to find a concept to give the work shape, a throughline to serve as a unifying theme.

Most of the songs here are well known and traditional, so I decided the setting should be historical. My interest in all things theatrical and my love of eighteenth-century garb led me swiftly to the little theatre concept, which also gave me the chance to underline some of the absurdities contained in these witty rhymes. The characters fell into place as principals, chorus, and stage assistants set in frames and against backdrops. Once I had the concept established, it allowed me to let even the characters in a landscape or a room take on a staged quality.

With each song I looked for a key moment, a clue word, to spark an idea. The footnote gave me the idea for "Yankee Doodle." This symbolic American is first humiliated by British soldiers, but returns triumphantly to cheering crowds as George Washington on the next page. In "Mary, Mary" the word "contrary" was my clue, and in "See-Saw, Marjorie Daw" the subtext seemed more about Jack's rising and falling misfortunes than see-sawing.

I struggled with pleasure for over a year to complete these illustrations. I hope singers and performers everywhere will enjoy them, and the words and music, for many years to come.

Anita Lobel

Guitar Chords

× = Don't play this string

Roman Numerals = fret numbers ●—● = bar with first finger

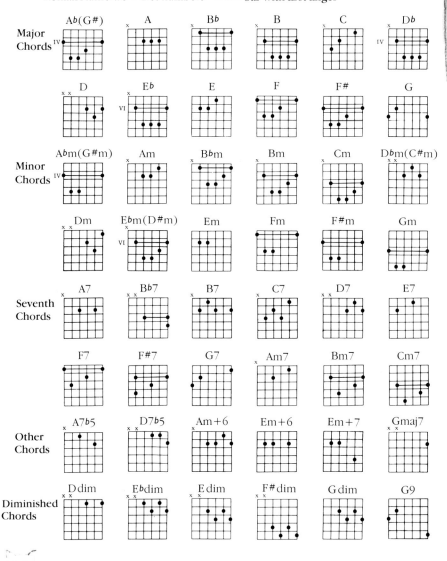

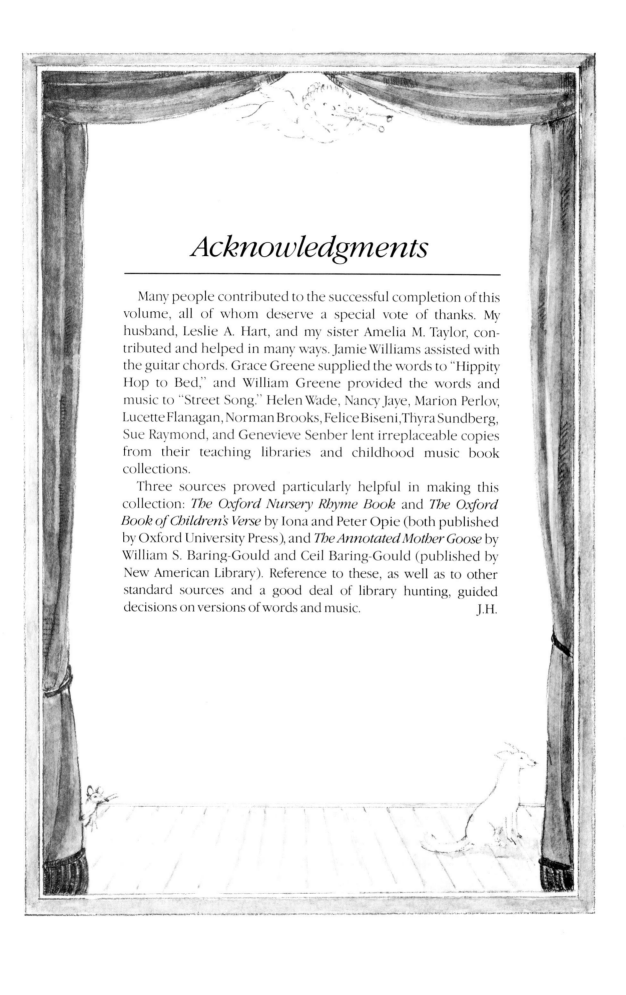

Acknowledgments

Many people contributed to the successful completion of this volume, all of whom deserve a special vote of thanks. My husband, Leslie A. Hart, and my sister Amelia M. Taylor, contributed and helped in many ways. Jamie Williams assisted with the guitar chords. Grace Greene supplied the words to "Hippity Hop to Bed," and William Greene provided the words and music to "Street Song." Helen Wade, Nancy Jaye, Marion Perlov, Lucette Flanagan, Norman Brooks, Felice Biseni, Thyra Sundberg, Sue Raymond, and Genevieve Senber lent irreplaceable copies from their teaching libraries and childhood music book collections.

Three sources proved particularly helpful in making this collection: *The Oxford Nursery Rhyme Book* and *The Oxford Book of Children's Verse* by Iona and Peter Opie (both published by Oxford University Press), and *The Annotated Mother Goose* by William S. Baring-Gould and Ceil Baring-Gould (published by New American Library). Reference to these, as well as to other standard sources and a good deal of library hunting, guided decisions on versions of words and music.   J.H.

All the Pretty Little Horses

This gentle, beautiful song has long been a well-loved lullaby in the Deep South.

Hush, Little Baby

This engaging song appears to be an old American version of a still older traditional English lullaby.

1. If that diamond ring turns brass,
Papa's going to buy you a looking glass.
2. If that looking glass gets broke,
Papa's going to buy you a billy goat.
3. If that billy goat won't pull,
Papa's going to buy you a cart and bull.

4. If that cart and bull turns over,
Papa's going to buy you a dog named Rover.
5. If that dog named Rover won't bark,
Papa's going to buy you a horse and cart.
6. If that horse and cart fall down,
You'll still be the sweetest baby in town!

Hippity Hop to Bed

As a going-to-bed song, this is hard to beat.

G. Greene
Casual, at first

J. Hart

Hip - pi - ty hop to bed, ____ I'd rath - er stay up in -

stead. But! When Dad - dy says "must," There's no - thing else, just

Hip - pi - ty, hop - pi - ty, Hip - pi - ty, hop - pi - ty, Hip - pi - ty, hop - pi - ty,

Hip - pi - ty, hip - pi - ty, hop! ____ To bed! ____

Bye, Baby Bunting

One of the earliest lullabies. "Bunting" was a term of endearment originating in Scotland.

Gently rocking

Traditional Lullaby

Bye, ba — by bunt — ing, Dad — dy's gone a — hunt — ing,

Gone to get a rab - bit skin To wrap the ba — by bunt - ing in.

Bye, ba — by bunt — ing.

The Sandman Comes

Flowing

Traditional Lullaby

Eb   Bb   Eb

The sand - man comes, the sand - man comes, He

Eb   C7   Fm

brings such pret - ty snow - white sand, For ev' - ry child through -

G   Cm   Eb   Bb7   Eb

out the land, The sand - man comes.

Golden Slumbers

Traditional Lullaby

Gently rocking

Gol - den slum - bers kiss your eyes;

Smiles _ a - wake you when you rise; Sleep, pret - ty ba - by,

do _ not cry, _ And I will sing a lul - la - by,

Rock _ then, rock then, lul - la - by. _____

Lullaby

Words adapted by L. Hart from the German

Tenderly

Brahms

Lull - a - by, and good night, In the sky stars are bright; Round your head, flow - ers gay Scent your slum - bers till day. Close your eyes now and rest, May these hours be blest, Go to sleep now and rest, May these hours be blest.

Sleep, Baby, Sleep

Gently rocking

Traditional Lullaby

Sleep, ba - by, sleep, Thy fa - ther guards the sheep, Thy moth - er shakes the dream - land tree, And from it fall sweet dreams for thee, Sleep, ba - by, sleep, Sleep, ba - by, sleep. ____

Wee Willie Winkie

Traditional Lullaby
Adapted by J. Hart

Wee Wil - lie Win - kie runs through the town, Up - stairs, down - stairs, in his night - gown; Rap - ping at the win - dow, Cry - ing at the lock, Are the chil - dren all in bed? For now it's eight o' - clock!

Rockabye, Baby

Gently

Traditional Lullaby

Rock - a - bye, ba - by, on the tree top,

When the wind blows, the cra - dle will rock;

When the bough breaks, the cra - dle will fall, And

down will come ba - by, cra - dle and all.

Now the Day Is Over

This lovely old hymn is gentle and soothing, a good lullaby for a tired child.

Sabine Baring-Gould
Softly

Joseph Barnaby
Lullaby

Now the day is o-ver, Night is draw-ing nigh;

R.H. Shad-ows of the eve-ning Steal a-cross the sky.

Father, give the weary
Calm and sweet repose;
With thy tender blessing,
May our eyelids close.

The Caterpillar

Emilie Poulsson
Brightly

Cornelia C. Roeske
Finger Play

Fuz - zy lit - tle cat - er - pil - lar, Crawl - ing, crawl - ing on the ground, Fuz - zy lit - tle cat - er - pil - lar, No - where, no - where to be found, Tho' we've looked and looked and hunt - ed, Ev - 'ry where a - round!

When the little caterpillar
Found his furry coat too tight,
Then a snug cocoon he made him,
Spun of silk so soft and light;
Rolled himself away within it–
Slept there day and night.

See how this cocoon is stirring–
Now a little head we spy.
What! is this our caterpillar,
Spreading gorgeous wings to dry?
Soon the free and happy creature
Flutters gaily by.

The thumb, hiding in the fist, is the caterpillar, and the fist is the cocoon.
Move the thumb in the fist to act out verses one and two. On the third verse,
cross your thumbs and spread fingers wide to indicate the butterfly drying
its wings. Move your fingers and the "happy creature flutters gaily by."

22

Here Are My Lady's Knives and Forks

J. Hart
Finger Play

Traditional Nursery Rhyme

Here are my la-dy's knives and forks, Here is my la-dy's ta - ble; Here is my la-dy's look - ing glass, And here is my ba - by's cra - dle.

For this finger play: Interlock fingers with palms turned up to indicate the knives and forks. Fingers still interlocked, turn palms down, and backs of hands become the table. To suggest the looking glass, form a circle by touching the index fingers and thumbs together. Rest one hand lightly on top of the other, palms up, and rock arms back and forth to make the cradle.

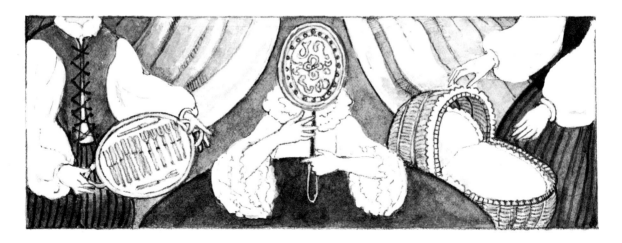

Here Is the Church

J. Hart
Finger Play

Traditional Nursery Rhyme

Here is the church, here is the stee-ple; O-pen the door, see all the peo-ple.

Interlock fingers, down. Raise two index fingers for steeple. Turn fingers up to see all the people—children like to see them in motion, wiggling.

Knock at the Door

J. Hart
Finger Play

Traditional Nursery Rhyme

Knock at the door, Peep in; Lift up the latch And walk in.

As you sing to a little one, lightly touch his forehead as you sing "Knock at the door." On "Peep in," gently touch the eyelids. On "Lift up the latch" touch the nose, and on "Walk in," touch the baby's mouth.

This Little Pig

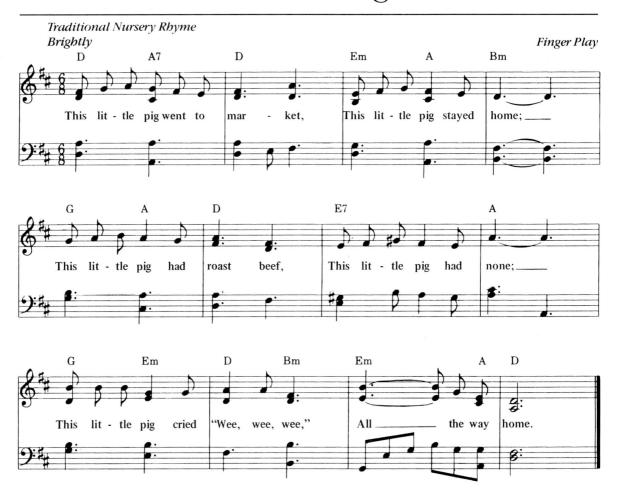

Traditional Nursery Rhyme
Brightly

Finger Play

This lit - tle pig went to mar - ket, This lit - tle pig stayed home;

This lit - tle pig had roast beef, This lit - tle pig had none;

This lit - tle pig cried "Wee, wee, wee," All the way home.

Take hold of the baby's big toe for the first line; then on to the others in turn, reaching the little toe, which is vigorously waggled to "Wee, wee, wee!" You may have to repeat the whole procedure quite a number of times.

Pat-a-Cake

Traditional Nursery Rhyme
Brightly

Finger Play

Pat - a - cake, pat - a - cake, ba - ker's man, Bake me a cake ___ as

fast as you can. Pat it and shape it and

mark it with B, And bake it in the o - ven for Ba - by and me.

Incey Wincey Spider

Each child puts left first finger against right thumb, then left thumb against right first finger, continuing this twist as hands are raised "up the spout." For "down came the rain," hands are lowered with all fingers dropping. For "out came the sun," children move hands to describe a large circle. Then repeat climbing action.

Where Is Thumbkin?

Finger Play

Lively

Where is thumb - kin, where is thumb - kin? Here I am,

here I am, How are you this morn - ing? Ver - y well, I thank you,

Run a - way, run a - way.

Where is pointer, etc.
Where is tall man, etc.
Where is ring man, etc.
Where is pinkie, etc.
Where are all the men, etc.

Put your hands behind your back. On "Here I am," bring out the right hand, closed, with the thumb up; then the left hand, closed, with the thumb up. On "How are you this morning?" right thumb wiggles; on "Very well, I thank you," left thumb wiggles. On "Run away," put right hand behind back, then left hand behind back.

Follow the same procedure for all the other fingers. On "Where are all the men?" the whole hand comes out, wiggling fingers and making hand movements as you sing "How are you this morning?" and "Very well, we thank you." On "Run away, run away," the hands return behind the back.

Children learn this at once, and enjoy doing it with their friends.

Sing a Song of Sixpence

Scholars have advanced many explanations for the references in this song. It may even include a reference to the first English printed Bible. Today, children are fascinated by the unexpected twists the words take-especially the ending!

Brightly

Traditional Song

Sing a song of six - pence, a pock - et full of rye,

Four and twen - ty black - birds baked in a pie;

When the pie was o - pened, the birds be - gan to sing,

Was - n't that a dain - ty dish to set be - fore the King?

The King was in his counting house, counting out his money,
The Queen was in the parlour, eating bread and honey,
The maid was in the garden, hanging out the clothes,
Along came a blackbird and nipped off her nose!

Pop! Goes the Weasel

Brightly

Traditional Song

All a-round the cob-bler's bench, The mon - key chased the wea - sel; The
mon - key thought 'twas all ____ in fun, Pop! goes the wea - sel.
I've no time to sit __ and sigh, No pa - tience to wait till time __ goes by;
Kiss me quick, I'm off, good - bye, Pop! goes the wea - sel.

The North Wind Doth Blow

Traditional Song
Arranged by J. Hart

With expression

The north wind doth blow, And we shall have snow, And what will the rob - in do then, poor thing? He'll sit in the barn, and keep him - self warm, And hide his head un - der his wing, poor thing!

The Muffin Man

Traditional Song

Smoothly

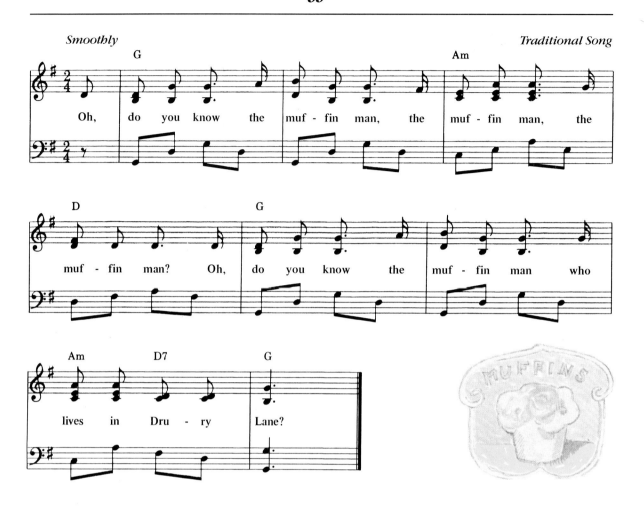

Oh, do you know the muf-fin man, the muf-fin man, the muf-fin man? Oh, do you know the muf-fin man who lives in Dru-ry Lane?

Oh, yes, we know the muffin man, the muffin man, the muffin man,
Oh, yes, we know the muffin man who lives in Drury Lane.

Little Tommy Tucker

Wandering performers sang for their suppers at inns and taverns. They were the originators of many nursery rhymes.

Whimsically

Traditional Song

Lit - tle Tom - my Tuck - er Sings—— for his sup - per,

What shall he sing for? White bread and but - ter. How shall he cut it with-

out an - y knife? How shall he mar - ry—— with - out an - y wife?

35

Little Jack Horner

Traditional Song

Simply

Lit - tle Jack Hor - ner sat in a cor - ner, Eat - ing his Christ - mas pie; _____ He put in his thumb, and pulled out a plum, And said, "What a good boy am I!" _____

See-Saw, Marjorie Daw

Lilting

Traditional Song

See - saw, Mar - jo - rie Daw, Jack - y shall have a new mas - ter; He shall have but a pen - ny a day, Be - cause he won't work an - y fas - ter.

Mary, Mary, Quite Contrary

Mary may have been Mary, Queen of Scots. The "pretty maids"
would have been her ladies-in-waiting.

Mary, Mary, quite con - tra - ry, how does your gar - den grow? With

sil - ver bells and cock - le shells, and pret - ty maids all in a row.

Jack and Jill

Traditional Song

Briskly

C   Am   Dm7   G   C

Jack and Jill went up the hill, To fetch a pail of wa - ter;

C7   F   Dm   G7   C

Jack fell down and broke his crown, And Jill came tum - bling af - ter.

Little Miss Muffet

*It is likely that this song had political origins, like so many old
nursery favourites, but the references are obscure now. That
children still enjoy the song is indisputable.*

Whimsically

Traditional Song

Lit - tle Miss Muf - fet sat on a tuf - fet,

Eat - ing her curds and whey; _____ A - long came a spi - der, and

sat down be - side her, And fright - ened Miss Muf - fet a - way. _____

Doctor Foster

This song is thought to refer to a visit by Edward the First to the city of Gloucester, during which his horse sank so deeply into mud that planks had to be laid to enable the royal rider to get out. King Edward was not pleased.

L. Hart
Traditional Nursery Rhyme

Pompously

Doc - tor Fos - ter went to Glou - cester In a show - er of

rain, He stepped in a pud - dle right up to his mid - dle, And

nev - er went there a - gain.

There Was an Old Woman

Gaily   *Traditional Song*

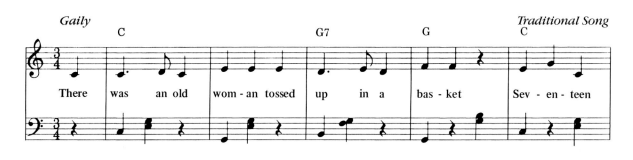

There was an old wom-an tossed up in a bas-ket Sev - en - teen

times as high as the moon. And where was she go - ing, I

could - n't but ask it, For in her hand she car - ried a broom. "Old

woman, old woman, old woman," said I, "Oh whither, oh whither, oh whither so high?" "To sweep the cobwebs off the sky." "Shall I go with you?" "Aye, by and by."

Over in the Meadow

Traditional Song

Smoothly

O - ver in the mead - ow, in the sand, in the sun, Lived an old ___ moth - er frog ___ and her lit - tle frog - gie one. "Croak!" said the moth - er; "I croak," said the one, So they croaked and they croaked in the sand, in the sun.

Over in the meadow, in the stream so blue,
Lived an old mother fish and her little fishies two.
"Swim!" said the mother; "We swim," said the two,
So they swam and they swam in the stream so blue.

Over in the meadow, on a branch of the tree,
Lived an old mother bird and her little birdies three.
"Sing!" said the mother; "We sing," said the three,
So they sang and they sang on a branch of the tree.

Rub-a-Dub-Dub

Rollicking

Traditional Song

Rub - a - dub - dub, three men in a tub, And who do you think they be?_____ The butch - er, the bak - er, the can - dle - stick mak - er,

Run them down, run them down, Rogues! All three.

I Love Little Pussy

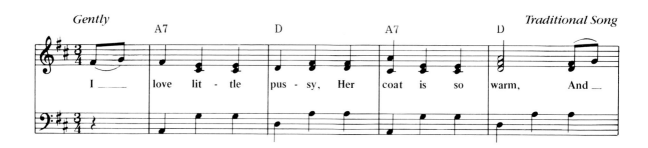

I'll sit by the fire
And give her some food,
And pussy will love me
Because I am good

Baa, Baa, Black Sheep

This song probably originated as a protest against the amount of wool that went to the king and the rich nobility. The rhyme has changed little in two hundred years.

Lightly

Traditional Song

Baa, baa, black sheep, have you an - y wool? Yes, sir, yes, sir, three bags full; One for my mas - ter, one for my dame, But none for the lit - tle boy who lives in the lane.

Simple Simon

With a steady beat   *Traditional Song*

Sim - ple Si - mon met a pie - man Go - ing to the fair. Said

Sim - ple Si - mon to the pie - man, "Let me taste your ware."

Said the man to Sim - ple Si - mon, "Show me first your pen - ny." Said

Sim - ple Si - mon to the pie - man, "In - deed, I have not an - y."

Rain, Rain

Universal Folk Melody

Pianists - try this or improvise your own variation:

Pussy Cat, Pussy Cat

Traditional Song

Smoothly

Pus - sy cat, pus - sy cat, where have you been? I've been to Lon - don to vis - it the Queen. Pus - sy cat, pus - sy cat, what did you there? I fright - ened a lit - tle mouse un - der her chair.

Hickory Dickory Dock

Back to the days of grandfather clocks! One of the oldest limericks.

With a steady beat

Traditional Song

Hick - or - y dick - or - y dock, The mouse ___ ran up ___ the

clock. The clock struck one, The mouse ran down,

Hick-or - y dick - or - y dock.

Ride a Cock Horse

With spirit

Traditional Song

Ride a cock horse to Ban - bur - y Cross, To see a fine la - dy up - on a white horse; Rings on her fin - gers and bells on her toes, She shall have mu - sic where - ev - er she goes.

Little Nut Tree

Lightly   Traditional Song

I had a little nut tree, noth-ing would it bear,

But a sil-ver nut-meg and a gold-en pear. The

King of Spain's daugh-ter came to vis-it me, And

all for the sake of my lit-tle nut tree.

Hark, Hark!

Traditional Song

Briskly

Hark, hark! The dogs do bark, Beg-gars are com-ing to town;

Some in rags, some in tags, And some in vel - vet gowns.

Hippity Hop to the Barber Shop

Traditional Song

Hip-pi-ty hop to the bar-ber shop, To buy a stick of can - dy.

One for you and one for me, And one for sis - ter An - nie.

Over the Hills and Far Away

Briskly

Traditional Song

Tom he was a pi-per's son, He learnt to play when he was young, And all the tune that he could play Was "O-ver the hills and far a-way." O-ver the hills and a great way off, The wind shall blow my top-knot off.

Goosey, Goosey, Gander

The event this song refers to has long since been forgotten, but the surprise in the last line keeps it endlessly popular with children.

Brightly   *Traditional Song*

Goo - sey, goo - sey, gan - der, whi - ther do you wan - der?

Up - stairs and down - stairs, and in my la - dy's cham - ber.

There I met an old man who would not say his prayers; So I

took him by the left leg and threw him down the stairs.

Mary Had a Little Lamb

Cheerily   *Traditional Song*

Ma - ry had a lit - tle lamb, lit - tle lamb, lit - tle lamb,

Ma - ry had a lit - tle lamb, its fleece was white as snow.

It followed her to school one day,
school one day, school one day,
It followed her to school one day,
which was against the rule.

And so the teacher turned it out,
turned it out, turned it out,
And so the teacher turned it out,
but still it lingered near.

It made the children laugh and play,
laugh and play, laugh and play,
It made the children laugh and play
to see a lamb at school.

What makes the lamb love Mary so?
Mary so, Mary so,
What makes the lamb love Mary so?
the eager children cry.

Why, Mary loves the lamb, you know,
lamb, you know, lamb, you know,
Why, Mary loves the lamb, you know,
the teacher did reply.

Merrily We Roll Along

(To the same music as *Mary Had a Little Lamb*)

Mer-ri-ly we roll a-long, roll a-long, roll a-long,
Mer-ri-ly we roll a-long, o'er the deep blue sea.

Polly, Put the Kettle On

Traditional Song

Lightly

Pol - ly, put the ket - tle on, Pol - ly, put the ket - tle on,

Pol - ly, put the ket - tle on, We'll all have tea.

Su - key, take it off a - gain, Su - key, take it off a - gain,

Su - key, take it off a - gain, They've all gone home.

Curly Locks

Scottish version of this old song begins with "Bonnie lass, bonnie lass."

Tenderly   *Traditional Song*

Cur - ly locks, cur - ly locks, Will you be mine? You shall not wash dish - es Nor yet feed the swine, But sit on a cush - ion and sew a fine seam; And feed up - on straw - ber - ries, su - gar and cream.

Lazy Mary

Firmly   *Traditional Song*

La - zy Ma - ry, will you get up, Will you get up, will you get up?

La - zy Ma - ry, will you get up, Will you get up to - day?

No, no, Mother, I won't get up,
I won't get up, I won't get up;
No, no, Mother, I won't get up,
I won't get up today!

Little Drops of Water

Lightly   *Traditional Song*

Lit - tle drops of wa - ter, Lit - tle grains — of sand,

Make the might - y o - cean, And the plea - sant land.

Little deeds of kindness,
Little words of love,
Help to make earth happy,
Like the heaven above.

Twinkle, Twinkle, Little Star

With spirit *Traditional Song*

Twin - kle, twin - kle, lit - tle star, How I won - der what you are,

Up a - bove the world so high, Like a dia - mond in the sky.

Twin - kle, twin - kle, lit - tle star, How I won - der what you are!

When the blazing sun is gone,
When he nothing shines upon,
Then you show your little light,
Twinkle, twinkle all the night.
Twinkle, twinkle little star,
How I wonder what you are!

Then the traveller in the dark
Thanks you for your tiny spark;
He could not see which way to go,
If you did not twinkle so.
Twinkle, twinkle, little star,
How I wonder what you are!

Little Bo-Peep

Little Bo-Peep fell fast asleep
And dreamed she heard them bleating;
But when she woke, 'twas all a joke.
For they were still a-fleeting.

Then up she took her little crook,
And vowed that she would find them;
What was her joy to see them there,
Wagging their tails behind them.

Lavender's Blue

Traditional Song

Lightly

Lav - en - der's blue, dil - ly, dil - ly, lav - en - der's green;

When I am King, dil - ly, dil - ly, you shall be Queen.

Who told you so, dil - ly, dil - ly, who told you so?

'Twas my own heart, dil - ly, dil - ly, that told me so.

Hey Diddle Diddle

Probably the best-known nonsense verse in the English language. It may originally have referred to Queen Elizabeth the First, who was fond of dancing in her chambers with members of her court.

Brightly   *Traditional Song*

Hey did - dle did - dle, The cat and the fid - dle, The

cow jumped o - ver the moon, _____ The lit - tle dog laughed _ to

see such sport, And the dish ran a - way with the spoon. _____

Cock-a-Doodle-Doo!

Cock-a-doodle-doo!
What is my dame to do?
Till master finds his fiddling stick
She'll dance without her shoe.

68

John Peel

"Ken" is an old word for "know."

With a lilt

Hunting Song

Do ye ken John Peel with his coat so gay, Do ye ken John Peel at the break of day, Do ye ken John Peel when he's far, far a - way, With his hounds and his horn in the morn - ing?

Little Boy Blue

Lightly

Traditional Song

Lit - tle Boy Blue, come blow ___ your horn, The sheep's in the mead - ow, the cow's in the corn. Where is the boy who looks af - ter the sheep? He's un - der the hay - stack, fast a - sleep.

Humpty Dumpty

Lively

Traditional Song

Humpty Dumpty sat on a wall, Humpty Dumpty had a great fall; All the King's horses and all the King's men Couldn't put Humpty together again.

Three Little Kittens

Traditional Song

Brightly

Three lit - tle kit - tens, they lost their mit - tens, And they be - gan to cry:_____ "Oh, moth - er dear, see here, see here, Our mit - tens we have lost!"_____ "What, lost your mit - tens? You naugh - ty kit - tens! Then you shall have no pie."_____ "Me - ow!_____ Me - ow!_____ Me - ow!_____ Me - ow!"

Three little kittens, they found their mittens,
And they began to cry:
"Oh, Mother dear, see here, see here,
Our mittens we have found!"
"What, found your mittens? You darling kittens!
Then you shall have some pie."
"Meow! Meow! Meow! Meow!"

Three little kittens put on their mittens
And soon ate up the pie.
"Oh, Mother dear, we greatly fear,
Our mittens we have soiled."
"What, soiled your mittens? You naughty kittens!"
And they began to sigh,
"Meow! Meow! Meow! Meow!"

Three little kittens, they washed their mittens,
And hung them up to dry.
"Oh, Mother dear, see here, see here,
Our mittens we have washed."
"What, washed your mittens? You darling kittens!
But I smell a mouse close by!
Hush! Hush! Hush! Hush!"

Old King Cole

Traditional Song

Rollicking

Old King Cole was a mer - ry old ____ soul, And a mer - ry old soul was he; He ____ called for his pipe, and he called for his bowl, And he called for his fid - dlers ____ three.

Ev - 'ry___ fid - dler___ had ___ a ___ fid - dle, and a ve - ry fine__ fid - dle had __ he;_____ Twee - dle dee, twee - dle dee, Went the fid - dlers ___ three, And __ mer - ry we __ will __ be.

Diddle, Diddle, Dumpling

"Diddle, diddle, dumpling" probably was the street cry of hot-dumpling sellers.

Playfully　　　　　　　　　　　　　　　　　　　　*Traditional Song*

Did - dle, did - dle, dump - ling, my son John, Went to bed with his

trous - ers on, One stock - ing off and one stock - ing on.

Did - dle, did - dle, dump - ling, my son John.

Five Little Chickadees

Lightly

American Singing Game

Verse: Five little chickadees peeping at the door, One flew a-way and then there were four; Chick-a-dee, chick-a-dee, hap-py and gay, Chick-a-dee, chick-a-dee, fly a-way.

Verse: Four little chickadees sitting on a tree,
　　　　One flew away and then there were three;
　　　　Chorus
Verse: Three little chickadees looking at you,
　　　　One flew away and then there were two;
　　　　Chorus
Verse: Two little chickadees sitting in the sun,
　　　　One flew away and then there was one;
　　　　Chorus
Verse: One little chickadee left all alone,
　　　　It flew away and then there were none;
　　　　Chorus

This can be a game with children acting out the verses and "flying" across the room, or it can be a finger play, with each finger representing a chickadee.

The Farmer in the Dell

Gaily

Traditional Singing Game

The farm - er in the dell, ___ The farm - er in the dell, ___ Heigh - ho, the der - ry - o, The farm - er in the dell. ___

The farmer takes a wife, etc.
The wife takes a child, etc.
The child takes a nurse, etc.
The nurse takes a dog, etc.
The dog takes a cat, etc.
The cat takes a rat, etc.
The rat takes the cheese, etc.
The cheese stands alone, etc.

Children form a circle with one child as "farmer" in the middle. They join hands and sing while dancing around the farmer. He chooses a wife to join him, etc. On the last verse the child chosen to be the cheese stands alone, and becomes the farmer for the next game.

The Mulberry Bush

With gusto   *Traditional Singing Game*

Here we go round the mul-ber-ry bush, the mul-ber-ry bush, the

mul-ber-ry bush. Here we go round the mul-ber-ry bush, so

ear-ly in the morn-ing.

This is the way we wash our clothes, etc.,
So early Monday morning.

This is the way we iron our clothes, etc.,
So early Tuesday morning.

This is the way we mend our clothes, etc.,
So early Wednesday morning.

This is the way we scrub the floor, etc.,
So early Thursday morning.

This is the way we sweep the house, etc.,
So early Friday morning.

This is the way we bake our bread, etc.,
So early Saturday morning.

This is the way we go to church, etc.,
So early Sunday morning.

Nuts in May

(To the same music as *The Mulberry Bush*)

1. Here we come gath'ring nuts in May,
   nuts in May, nuts in May,
   Here we come gath'ring nuts in May,
   all on a frosty morning.

2. Whom will you have for nuts in May,
   nuts in May, nuts in May,
   Whom will you have for nuts in May,
   all on a frosty morning?

3. We will have Mary for nuts in May,
   nuts in May, nuts in May,
   We will have Mary for nuts in May,
   all on a frosty morning.

4. Whom will you send to fetch her away,
   fetch her away, fetch her away,
   Whom will you send to fetch her away,
   all on a frosty morning?

5. We will send Betty to fetch her away,
   fetch her away, fetch her away,
   We will send Betty to fetch her away,
   all on a frosty morning.

Children form two lines, holding hands; they advance toward each other, then fall back. One line sings verses 1, 3, 5, and the other sings 2, 4 in reply. The leader, at the end of the first line, fetches a child in the opposite line, on cue, and both return. When all but one are in the first line, the child who is left becomes leader and brings the others back to that side. Children's actual names are used.

Bingo

American Folk Song

Sing through once. Then, singing faster each time through, clap once instead of singing "B," twice instead of singing "B-I," and so forth.

Bluebird

Briskly

Blue - bird, blue - bird, Through my — win - dow, Blue - bird, blue - bird,

Through my — win - dow, Blue - bird, blue - bird, Through my — win - dow,

Oh, John - ny, I am tir - ed.

Take a little girl, tap her on the shoulder,
Take a little girl, tap her on the shoulder,
Take a little girl, tap her on the shoulder,
Oh, Johnny, I am tired.

Children make a circle, hands raised to form arches. A child chosen to be a bluebird skips in and out the arches until verse two, when she chooses a second bluebird by tapping someone in the circle on the shoulder. Repeat with two bluebirds, then four, etc., until everyone is a bluebird. All fall down to rest at the words "I am tired."

The Gallant Ship

Rollicking   *Traditional Singing Game*

Three times a-round went the gal-lant ship, And three times a-round went she; Oh, three times a-round went the gal-lant ship, And she sank to the bot-tom of the sea.

Children join hands in a circle. They all take sliding steps to the left, until "and she sank" when they jump in place; jumping and crouching on "to the bot-tom," and jumping again on "of the sea," coming to a sitting-on-heels position and trying not to fall over.

Go Round and Round the Village

Briskly

Traditional Singing Game

Go round and round the village, Go round and round the village, Go round and round the village, As we have done before.

Go in and out the window,
Go in and out the window,
Go in and out the window,
As we have done before.

Stand and face your partner,
Stand and face your partner,
Stand and face your partner,
As we have done before.

Follow me to London,
Follow me to London,
Follow me to London,
As we have done before.

Now shake his hand and leave him,
Now shake his hand and leave him,
Now shake his hand and leave him,
As we have done before.

Children stand in a circle, pretending to be houses in a village. One child is IT and runs around the village during the first verse. On the second verse, those in the circle raise their arms to make windows, and IT runs in and out. On the third verse, IT chooses a partner and they both bow. On the fourth verse, partners join hands and skip around the circle. They go back inside the circle on the fifth verse, shake hands, bow; and the second child becomes IT.

Clap Your Hands

With spirit

American Folk Song

Clap, clap, clap your hands, Clap your hands to - geth - er;

Clap, clap, clap your hands, Clap your hands to - geth - er.

La la la la la la la, La la la la la la,

La la la la la la la, Clap your hands to - geth - er!

mf   *crescendo*   *ff*

Sally, Go Round

Playfully

Traditional Singing Game

Sal - ly, go round the sun, —— Sal - ly, go round the moon, ——

Sal - ly, go round the chim - ney pots Ev - 'ry af - ter - noon. BUMP!

Children join hands in a circle and skip around to the left; at the word "bump"
they reverse and skip around to the right.

The Noble Duke of York

March time

Traditional Singing Game

Oh, the no-ble Duke of York, He had ten thou-sand men; He marched them up to the top of the hill, And marched them down a-gain.

Oh, when you're up you're up,
And when you're down you're down,
And when you're only halfway up,
You're neither up nor down.

Children form two lines, partners facing each other. While all are singing the first verse, the head couple marches to the foot of the set and back. On the second verse they join hands and swing around to the foot of the set again. The second couple now becomes the head couple.

A-Hunting We Will Go

(To the same music as *The Noble Duke of York*)

Oh, a-hunt-ing we will go,
A-hunt-ing we will go,
We'll catch a fox and put him in a box,
And then we'll let him go.

Oats, Peas, Beans

Traditional Singing Game

With gusto

Oats, peas, beans, and bar - ley grow, Oats, peas, beans, and bar - ley grow, Do you or I or an - y - one know How oats, peas, beans, and bar - ley grow?

First the farmer sows his seeds,
Then he stands and takes his ease,
Stamps his feet, and claps his hand,
And turns around to view the land.

Waiting for a partner,
Waiting for a partner,
Open the ring and take one in,
And then we'll dance and gaily sing.

On the first verse, children form a circle, join hands, skip around to the left. One child stands in the centre as the farmer.

He acts out the words of the second verse, sowing seed, turning around, and shading his eyes to view the land.

On the third verse, he chooses a partner; all join hands and skip around outside the farmer and his partner.

Another child becomes the farmer when the song begins again.

Skip to My Lou

American Play Party Game

Gaily

Chorus F

Skip, skip, skip to my Lou, Skip, skip, skip to my Lou,

Skip, skip, skip to my Lou, Skip to my Lou, my dar - ling!

Verse F

Lost my part - ner, what - 'll I do? Lost my part - ner, what - 'll I do?

F   Gm   F   C7   F

Lost my part - ner, what - 'll I do? Skip to my Lou, my dar - ling!

Chorus

Verse: I'll find another one, prettier, too,
I'll find another one, prettier, too,
I'll find another one, prettier, too,
Skip to my Lou, my darling!

Chorus

Verse: Can't get a red bird, blue bird'll do,
Can't get a red bird, blue bird'll do,
Can't get a red bird, blue bird'll do,
Skip to my Lou, my darling!

Chorus

Verse: Flies in the sugar bowl, shoo, shoo, shoo,
Flies in the sugar bowl, shoo, shoo, shoo,
Flies in the sugar bowl, shoo, shoo, shoo,
Skip to my Lou, my darling!

Children stand with partners in a circle; an extra child is in the centre. All sing and clap to the chorus. On "Lost my partner," the child in the centre chooses one in the circle, and in skating formation (crossed hands) they skip around the outside of the circle, the others clapping.

All skip around to the left on the chorus.

The child whose partner was taken sings "I'll get another one," chooses another, and takes his turn around the circle.

This sequence continues until the end of the dance.

Looby Loo

Joyfully

Traditional Singing Game

Chorus

Here we go loo-by loo, Here we go loo-by light, Here we go loo-by loo, All on a Sat-ur-day night. I put my right hand in, I put my right hand out, I give my right hand a shake, shake, shake, And turn my-self a-bout.

Chorus

Verse: I put my left hand in, etc.

Chorus

Verse: I put my right foot in, etc.

Chorus

Verse: I put my left foot in, etc.

Chorus

Verse: I put my whole self in, etc.

On the chorus, children join hands in a circle and skip to the centre and back, then follow the directions as they sing them.

Gogo

English version by Margaret Marks *Singing Game from Kenya* *As sung by Mary Okari*
                                                                   Arranged by J. Hart

Children may want to organize their own Halloween parade. *Gogo* is a good
song to sing as the children, wearing masks, walk in "funny ways" as they
"hump and clump about."

Rig-a-Jig-Jig

Joyfully

American Play Party Game

As I was walk-ing down the street, down the street,

down the street, A pret-ty {girl / boy} I chanced to meet, Heigh-

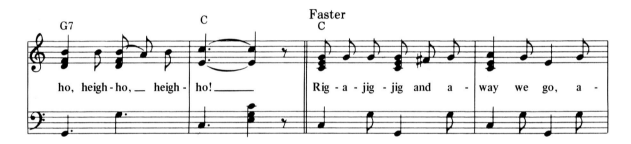

ho, heigh-ho, __ heigh-ho! ____ Rig-a-jig-jig and a-way we go, a-

Faster

way we go, a-way we go; Rig-a-jig-jig and a-

way we go, Heigh-ho, heigh-ho, ____ heigh-ho! ____

Children form two circles, one inside the other. On the verse one walks around clockwise, the other counterclockwise, both singing. On the last "Heigh-ho" before the chorus they stop, face the nearest child in the other circle, take hands, and skip around during the chorus. Then they drop hands and continue the game.

94

I'm a Little Teapot

Humorously   *Traditional Action Song*

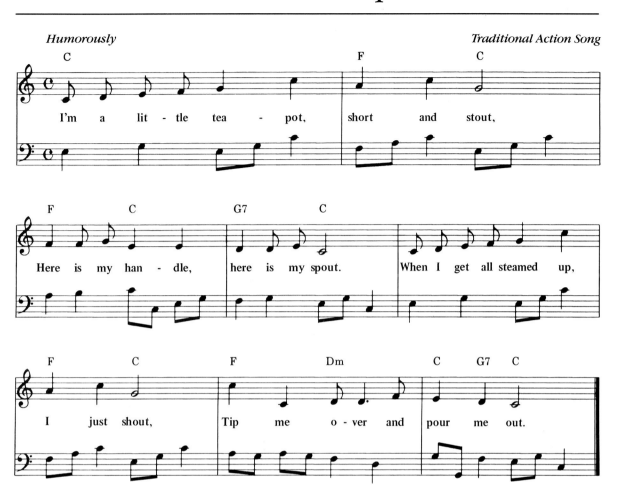

I'm a lit - tle tea - pot, short and stout,

Here is my han - dle, here is my spout. When I get all steamed up,

I just shout, Tip me o - ver and pour me out.

Give the following directions for acting out the words:

"Left hand on your hip for the handle, right hand on your shoulder for the spout, don't lean too far over to pour out!"

Did You Ever See a Lassie?

Gaily

Traditional Singing Game

Did you ev - er see a lass - ie, a lass - ie, a

lass - ie, Did you ev - er see a lass - ie go this way and

that? Go this way and that way, And this way and that way, Did you

ev - er see a lass - ie Go this way and that?

Children form a circle with one player in the centre as IT. They skip to the left until "this way and that," when the child who is IT originates a rhythmic pattern such as clapping, stamping, swaying, which the others imitate. The centre child chooses another IT and the game continues. (If a boy is IT the word "laddie" is used.)

Three White Gulls

English words by Marguerite Wilkinson
Smoothly

Italian Folk Song

There are three ____ white gulls ____ a - fly - ing, There are three ____ white gulls ____ a - fly - ing, There are three ____ white gulls a - fly - ing ____ By the sea they cry, by the sea they cry, by the sea they cry.

In the sea they dip their soft wings,
In the sea they dip their soft wings,
In the sea they dip their soft wings–
Then soar to the sky, then soar to the sky,
Then soar to the sky.

When children have learned this song, they will enjoy moving around the room. The rise and fall of the melody suggests the movement of the gulls' wings.

See the Pony Galloping, Galloping

To Market, to Market

With spirit   *Traditional Singing Game*

To market, to market, to buy a fat pig;
Home again, home again, jig-get-ty jig. To
market, to market, to buy a fat hog;
Home again, home again, jig-get-ty jog.

To market, to market, to buy a plum cake;
Home again, home again, market is late.
To market, to market, to buy a plum bun;
Home again, home again, market is done.

A Tisket, a Tasket

Traditional Singing Game

Children join hands in a circle; one child chosen to be IT holds a hand-kerchief. While all are singing, IT skips around the outside of the circle. On the last "I lost it," IT drops the handkerchief behind the nearest child. In the same direction he or she has been going, IT races around the circle; the child behind whom the handkerchief has been dropped races around the circle in the opposite direction; the last one to get back to the handkerchief is now IT and the game begins again.

Little Sally Waters

Playfully

Traditional Singing Game

Lit - tle Sal - ly Wa - ters, sit - ting in the sun,

Cry - ing and weep - ing, ___ lone-some lit - tle one. Rise, Sal - ly, rise;

wipe off your eyes; Fly to the East, Sal - ly, Fly to the West, Sal - ly,

Fly to the one you love the ve - ry best.

The first Sally sits in the centre of the circle and acts out the words as the other children sing. On cue, she rises, "flies to the East" and "flies to the West." The player she goes to on the last line becomes the next Sally, and the game goes on until all have had a turn. Children love to act this out, pretending to weep and then to fly.

Bow Belinda

American Play Party Game

Playfully

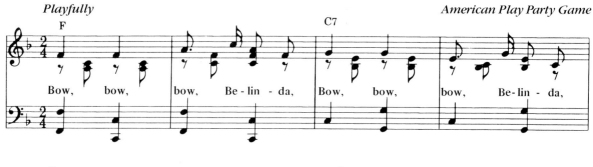

Right hand up, Oh, Belinda,
Right hand up, Oh, Belinda,
Right hand up, Oh, Belinda,
Won't you be my darling?

Left hand up, Oh, Belinda,
Left hand up, Oh, Belinda,
Left hand up, Oh, Belinda,
Won't you be my darling?

Both hands up, Oh, Belinda,
Both hands up, Oh, Belinda,
Both hands up, Oh, Belinda,
Won't you be my darling?

Shake that big foot shy all around her,
Shake that big foot shy all around her,
Shake that big foot shy all around her,
Won't you be my darling?

Promenade all, Oh, Belinda,
Promenade all, Oh, Belinda,
Promenade all, Oh, Belinda,
Won't you be my darling?

Boys line up in a row, facing equal number of girls in a row, a few feet apart.

On "Bow, bow, bow, Belinda," boys bow, girls bow or curtsy to facing partners.

On "Right hand up," partners advance, take named hand, turn around each other and back to places. This is repeated for left hand and both hands as sung.

On "Shake that big foot," all fold hands across chest, pass around partners back to back (do-si-do), and return to places.

On "Promenade all," head couple make arch with arms. Last couple take hands, march up between rows, under arch, separate, and return down outside. Remaining couples follow as soon as possible. Head couple separate and follow to become new bottom couple.

Five-year-olds love and can do this "longways" dance.

Jack, Be Nimble

For centuries, jumping over a candle has been a sport and a way of telling fortunes.

Briskly

Traditional Singing Game

Jack, be nim - ble, Jack, be quick, Jack, jump o - ver the can - dle stick.

Pease Porridge Hot

This is a clapping game, played by children on cold days to keep their hands warm.

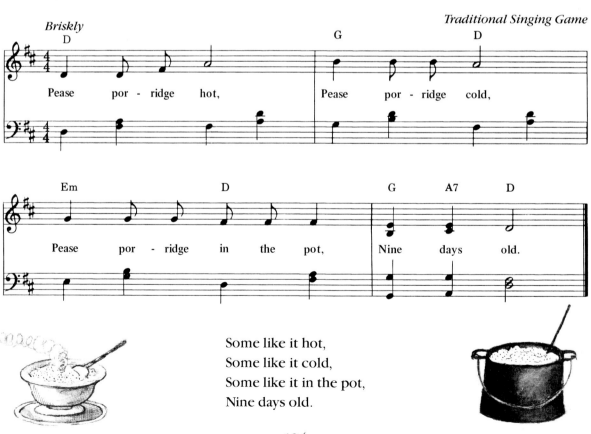

Briskly

Traditional Singing Game

Pease por - ridge hot, Pease por - ridge cold,

Pease por - ridge in the pot, Nine days old.

Some like it hot,
Some like it cold,
Some like it in the pot,
Nine days old.

London Bridge

Some scholars claim that this song stems from actual destruction of the bridge in the eleventh century by invading Norsemen.

Smoothly   *Traditional Singing Game*

Lon - don Bridge is fall - ing down, fall - ing down, fall - ing down,
Lon - don Bridge is fall - ing down, my fair la - dy.

Build it up with iron bars, etc.
Iron bars will bend and break, etc.
Build it up with pins and needles, etc.
Pins and needles rust and bend, etc.
Build it up with gravel and stone, etc.
Gravel and stone will wash away, etc.

Two players form the bridge by joining hands with both arms stretched upward. The other players march under the arch in single file. On "my fair lady" the arch falls, capturing a player who is asked to choose gold or silver, and then lines up behind whichever of the arch-makers represents that metal. When all players have been caught, the two lines have a tug of war.

105

Here Stands a Redbird

Joyfully

American Singing Game

Here stands a red-bird, Tra-la-la-la-la Here stands a red-bird,

Tra-la-la-la-la Rice, sug-ar and tea!

One child in the centre of the circle makes birdlike hopping, flying, pecking, or turning motions which the others imitate, and then selects a new Redbird.

Ring-a-Ring o'Roses

Traditional Singing Game

Lightly

Ring - a - ring a' ro - ses, A po - cket full of po - sies, A-
ti - shoo! A - ti - shoo! We all fall down.

Children join hands in a circle and skip to the left while singing. On "all fall down," be sure they let go of each other's hands and fall down as easily as possible.

Sur le Pont d'Avignon

Every year the people of Avignon, a beautiful city in southern France,
gather on their famous bridge, built by the Romans, to dance.

Joyfully

French Folk Song, Dance

Chorus

Sur le pont d'A - vi - gnon l'on y dan - se, l'on y dan - se;

Sur le pont d'A - vi - gnon l'on y dan - se, tout en rond.

Verse: Les mesdames font comme ci,
Et puis encore comme ça.

Sur le pont d'Avignon
l'on y danse, tout en rond.

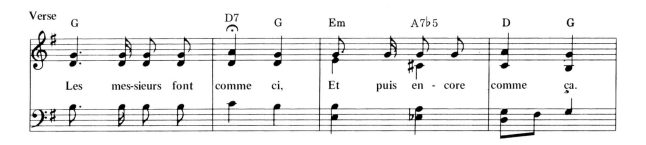

Verse

Les mes-sieurs font comme ci, Et puis en-core comme ça.

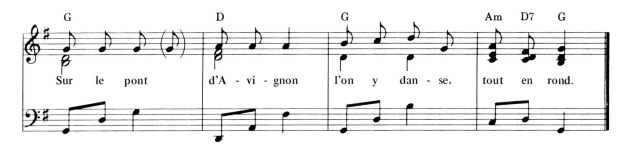

Sur le pont d'A - vi - gnon l'on y dan - se, tout en rond.

English translation

On the bridge at Avignon
They are dancing, they are dancing;
On the bridge at Avignon
They are dancing, all around.
Gentlemen go this way,
Then again go that way.
On the bridge at Avignon
They are dancing, all around.

On the bridge at Avignon
They are dancing, they are dancing;
On the bridge at Avignon
They are dancing, all around.
Ladies now go this way,
Then again go that way.
On the bridge at Avignon
They are dancing, all around.

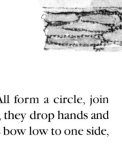

Each boy chooses a partner; the girl stands on the right. All form a circle, join hands, and skip to the right during the chorus. On the verse, they drop hands and face each other; On "Les messieurs font comme ci," the boys bow low to one side, then to the other.

Repeat the chorus.

On the second verse, girls bow to one side, then to the other, on "Les mesdames font comme ci." Then, on "Et puis encore comme ça," girls take one step to the left and resume the dance with a new partner.

Billy Boy

Irish-American Song

Lightly

Oh, ___ where ___ have you been, Bil - ly Boy, Bil - ly Boy? Oh, ___ where have you been, charm - ing Bil - ly? I have been to seek a wife, She's the joy ___ of my life, She's a young thing and can - not leave her moth - er. ___

Did she ask you to come in, Billy Boy, Billy Boy?
Did she ask you to come in, charming Billy?
Yes, she asked me to come in,
There's a dimple in her chin,
She's a young thing and cannot leave her mother.

Can she make a cherry pie, Billy Boy, Billy Boy?
Can she make a cherry pie, charming Billy?
She can make a cherry pie,
Quick as a cat can wink its eye,
She's a young thing and cannot leave her mother.

How old is she, Billy Boy, Billy Boy?
How old is she, charming Billy?
Three times six and four times seven,
Twenty-eight and eleven;
She's a young thing and cannot leave her mother.

The Bear Went Over the Mountain

The amiable quality of this song's words and tune enchants children.
Its origin is unknown.

American Traditional Song

Do Your Ears Hang Low?

A camp song from the days of the American Revolution. Children enjoy acting it out, especially wiggling their ears.

Humorously

American Revolutionary Folk Song

Do your ears hang low, do they wob-ble to and fro? Can you tie them in a knot, can you tie them in a bow? Can you fling them o-ver your shoul-der Like a Con-ti-nen-tal sol-dier, Do your ears hang low?

Where, Oh Where Has My Little Dog Gone?

Septimus Winter
American Minstrel Song

Oh where, oh where has my little dog gone? Oh where, oh where can he be? With his ears cut short and his tail cut long, Oh where, oh where is he?

114

Good Morning to You

"Happy Birthday" can also be sung to this melody.

Go Tell Aunt Rhody

One of the best known and loved of American folk songs, though the goose in some regions belongs to Aunt Betty, Aunt Nancy, or names other than Aunt Rhody. One may suspect that Auntie was not too distressed to have her feathers at last.

With feeling

American Traditional Song

Go tell Aunt Rho - dy, Go tell Aunt Rho - dy, Go tell Aunt Rho - dy, her old grey goose is dead. The

The one she's been saving,
The one she's been saving,
The one she's been saving,
To make a feather bed.

She died in the mill pond,
She died in the mill pond,
She died in the mill pond,
Standing on her head.

Street Song

*A song heard in Chicago, circa 1917. Many changes can be made –
going to the grocery or bakery or any other shop, calling for your
other friends besides Willie – but make the E-I-O loud and clear, so
he'll hear you in the next block.*

W. Greene
With gusto

American Folk Song

Up to the bar-ber shop I go, I can-not stay an-y long - er, For if I do my moth-er will say I played with the boys on the cor - ner. E - I - O for Wil - lie, E - I - O for Wil - lie; Won't you come, Won't you come, Won't you come and play with me?

Old MacDonald Had a Farm

Bouncy

Traditional Song

Old Mac-Don-ald had a farm, E - I - E - I - O! And
on this farm he had a dog, E - I - E - I - O! With a

And on this farm he had some ducks,
E-I-E-I-O!
With a quack, quack here, and a quack, quack there,
Here a quack, there a quack, ev'ry where a quack, quack,

With a bow-wow here, and a bow-wow there,
Here a bow, there a bow, ev'ry where a bow-wow,
Old MacDonald had a farm, E-I-E-I-O!

Continue with animals and their sounds:
Chick—chick, chick here, etc.
Cow—moo, moo here, etc.
Pig—oink, oink here, etc.
Horse—neigh, neigh here, etc.
Cat—meow, meow here, etc.

This is a cumulative song, and can be continued until all the animals of the
farmyard have been named.

There's a Little Wheel A-Turning

Lyrically

American Spiritual

There's a lit-tle wheel a-turn-ing in my heart, _____ There's a lit-tle wheel a-turning in my heart. In my heart _____ In my heart _____ There's a lit-tle wheel a-turn-ing in my heart.

There's a little song a-singing in my heart,
There's a little song a-singing in my heart.
In my heart–In my heart–
There's a little song a-singing in my heart.

Oh, I feel so very happy in my heart,
I feel so very happy in my heart.
In my heart–In my heart–
I feel so very happy in my heart.

Roll Over

Humorously

American Folk Song

Ten in the bed, and the lit-tle one said, "Roll o-ver! Roll o-ver!" They all rolled o-ver and one fell out.

Nine in the bed, etc.
Eight in the bed, etc.
Seven in the bed, etc.
Six in the bed, etc.
Five in the bed, etc.
Four in the bed, etc.
Three in the bed, etc.
Two in the bed, etc.
One in the bed, and the little one said,
"Alone at last!"

Yankee Doodle

The famous tune was used by the British to make fun of the Americans
during the first part of the Revolution. But the Americans made
it their own in the later years of the war, and so has it been ever since.

With martial precision

English-American Folk Song

Verse

Yan - kee Doo - dle went to town, a - rid - ing on a po - ny, He

stuck a feath - er in his cap and called it mac - a - ro - ni!

Chorus

Yan - kee Doo - dle, keep it up, Yan - kee Doo - dle dan - dy;

Mind the mu - sic and the step, and with the girls be hand - y!

Verse: Father and I went down to camp,
Along with Captain Gooding,
And there we saw the men and boys
As thick as hasty pudding.
Chorus

Verse: And there was Captain Washington
Upon a slapping stallion,
A-giving orders to his men,
I guess there was a million.
Chorus

Verse: And there I saw a little keg,
The head was made of leather;
They knocked on it with little sticks
To call the folks together.
Chorus

Eletelephony

Laura Elizabeth Richards
With clarity

J. Hart

Once there was an el - e - phant, Who tried to use the tel - e - phant— No! No! I mean an el - e - phone Who tried to use ____ the tel - e - phone ____ (Dear me, I am not cer - tain quite That e - ven now ____ I've got it right.) ____

Oh, Susanna!

*One of the best-known American songs of all time. First performed
in a minstrel show in 1848, it became popular with the forty-niners
as they headed West, and has never lost its appeal.*

Stephen Collins Foster

Briskly

Verse

I___ come from Al - a - bam - a with my ban - jo on my

knee; I'm___ going to Lou' - si - an - a, my___

true love for to see. It ___ rained all night the day I left, The

weath - er it was dry; The ___ sun so hot I

froze to death, Su - san - na, don't you cry.

Chorus

Oh, Su - san - na! Oh, don't you cry for me, I___

come from Al - a - bam - a with my ban - jo on my knee.

Verse: I had a dream the other night
When everything was still;
I thought I saw Susanna come
A-walking down the hill.
The red, red rose was in her hand,
The tear was in her eye;
I said, "I come from Alabam',
Susanna, don't you cry."
Chorus

She'll Be Coming Round the Mountain

One of the earliest American railroad songs, this has many versions.

She'll be driving six white horses when she comes, (spoken) whoa, back, etc.

And we'll all sing "Hallelujah" when she comes, (spoken) oh, yes, etc.

Down by the Station

Today's children may never have seen a steam engine, but they enjoy puffing like locomotives and moving fists like pistons as they march around.

Briskly

American Folk Song

Down by the sta - tion, ear - ly in the morn - ing,

See the lit - tle puff - er - bil - lies all in a row;

See the en - gine dri - ver pull the lit - tle throt - tle,

Chug, Chug, Poof, Poof! Off we go!

The Bus Song

Joyfully

Adapted with new words by Tom Glazer

1. Children go up and down in their seats.
2. Hold arms out and imitate wipers by waving forearms.
3. Pull an imaginary hand-brake up three times to "roomp, roomp, roomp."
4. Tap thumb against forefinger three times (same hand) to "clink, clink, clink."
5. Describe circles with both hands to "round and round."
6. Rock arms as if holding a baby.

2. The wiper on the bus goes "Swish, swish, swish,
   Swish, swish, swish; swish, swish, swish."
   The wiper on the bus goes "Swish, swish, swish,"
   All around the town.

3. The brake on the bus goes "Roomp, roomp, roomp,
   Roomp, roomp, roomp; roomp, roomp, roomp!"
   The brake on the bus goes "Roomp, roomp, roomp,"
   All around the town.

4. The money in the bus goes "Clink, clink, clink,
   Clink, clink, clink; clink, clink, clink."
   The money in the bus goes "Clink, clink, clink,"
   All around the town.

5. The wheels on the bus go round and round,
   Round and round, round and round.
   The wheels on the bus go round and round,
   All around the town.

6. There's a baby on the bus goes "Wah, wah, wah,
   Wah, wah, wah; wah, wah, wah."
   There's a baby on the bus goes "Wah, wah, wah,"
   All around the town.

Working on the Railroad

With spirit   *American Traditional Song*

I've been work - ing on the rail - road, All the live - long

day, I've been work - ing on the rail - road, Just to

pass the time a - way; Don't you hear the whis - tle

blow - ing, Rise up so ear - ly in the morn;

Frère Jacques

Traditional Round

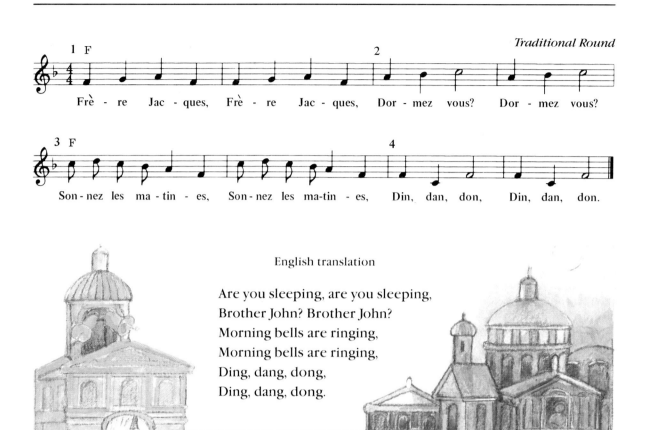

Frè - re Jac - ques, Frè - re Jac - ques, Dor - mez vous? Dor - mez vous?

Son - nez les ma - tin - es, Son - nez les ma - tin - es, Din, dan, don, Din, dan, don.

English translation

Are you sleeping, are you sleeping,
Brother John? Brother John?
Morning bells are ringing,
Morning bells are ringing,
Ding, dang, dong,
Ding, dang, dong.

Oh, How Lovely Is the Evening

Traditional Round

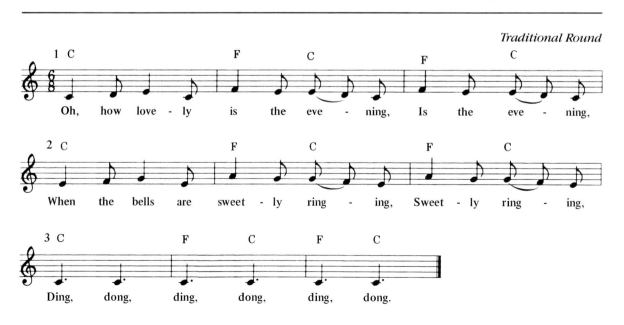

Oh, how love - ly is the eve - ning, Is the eve - ning,

When the bells are sweet - ly ring - ing, Sweet - ly ring - ing,

Ding, dong, ding, dong, ding, dong.

Row, Row, Row Your Boat

Traditional Round

1 C   2 C

Row,   row,   row your boat   Gent - ly down the   stream; _____

3 C

Mer - ri - ly,   mer - ri - ly,   mer - ri - ly,   mer - ri - ly,

4 C   G   C

Life   is   but   a   dream. _____

El Coquito (The Little Tree Toad)

Puerto Rican Lullaby

El Co - qui sings a sweet song at twi - light.

He is sing - ing as sleep comes to me. _____ When I

wake all a - lone in the moon - light, El Co - qui sings good -

night from the tree. _____ Co - qui, Co - qui, Co - qui, qui, qui,

qui. Co - qui, Co - qui, Co - qui, qui, qui, qui.

Mexican Counting Song

Mexican Folk Song

Brightly

U - no, dos, y tres, cua - tro, cin - co, seis,

Sie - te, o - cho, nue - ve, I can count to diez.

La la la la la La la la la la

La la la la la la! la la la!

English translation

Uno—one
Dos—two
Tres—three
Cuatro—four
Cinco—five
Seis—six
Siete—seven
Ocho—eight
Nueve—nine
Diez—ten

Lightly Row

German Folk Song

I Saw Three Ships

Joyfully

Traditional Song

I saw three ships come sail - ing by, A - sail - ing by, a - sail - ing by; I saw three ships come sail - ing by, On New— Year's Day in the morn - ing.

And what do you think was in them then,
Was in them then, was in them then?
And what do you think was in them then,
On New Year's Day in the morning?

Three pretty girls were in them then,
Were in them then, were in them then,
Three pretty girls were in them then,
On New Year's Day in the morning.

And one could whistle and one could sing,
And one could play the violin;
Such joy there was at my wedding,
On New Year's Day in the morning.

Hot Cross Buns

A street cry from London.

With gusto

Traditional Song

The Easter Bunny

An original song from the children in Sue Raymond's nursery school class in Westport, Connecticut.

Oh, the Eas - ter Bun - ny goes thump, thump, thump, The

Eas - ter Bun - ny goes jump, jump, jump, The Eas - ter Bun-ny's ears go

flop, flop, flop! Thump, thump, jump, jump, flop, flop, flop!

Thump, thump, jump, jump, flop, flop, flop!

L. H. staccato

141

Over the River and Through the Wood

Smoothly

American Traditional Song

O - ver the riv - er and through the wood, To grand - moth - er's house we go; _____ The horse knows the way to car - ry the sleigh, through white and drift - ed snow _____ O - ver the riv - er and

through the wood, Oh, how the wind does blow! It stings the toes and

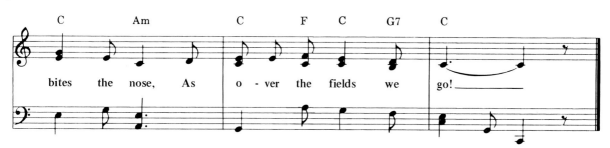

bites the nose, As o - ver the fields we go!

Over the river and through the wood,
Trot fast, my dapple grey!
Spring over the ground like a hunting hound,
For this is Thanksgiving Day!
Over the river and through the wood,
Now grandmother's cap I spy!
Hurrah for the fun! Is the pudding done?
Hurrah for the pumpkin pie!

Hanukkah Song

The Hebrew word Hanukkah means dedication. During the Festival of Lights, candles are lit on eight successive nights. The menorah is the candelabrum, the hora a traditional dance.

Jewish Folk Song

Joyfully

Oh, Ha-nuk-kah, Oh, Ha-nuk-kah, come light the me-no-rah.

Let's have a par - ty, we'll all dance the ho - ra.

Gath - er round the ta - ble, we'll give you a treat.

Shin - ing tops to play with and pan - cakes to eat. And

while we ___ are danc - ing, ___ the

can - dles are burn - ing ___ low;

One for each night, they will shed a sweet light To re-

mind us of days long a - go; ___

days long a - go.

Santa's Chimney

*My husband and I wrote this song when our children were little, and
it has become a part of our Christmas tradition.*

he'll have room for all of his toys; For a doll and a truck and a

car - riage and a train And a game and a bike and a sled and a plane, And a

drum to make a noise! Jump-in' jim - in - ey, San - ta's chim - in - ey,

Build it right a - way, So San - ta Claus can

vis - it us the good old - fash - ioned way! _____

Jingle Bells

*The words and music to this popular holiday song were written by
John Pierpont, a Unitarian minister who was born in 1785.*

Dash - ing through the snow, In a one - horse o - pen sleigh,

O'er the fields we go, laugh - ing all the way.

Bells on bob - tail ring, mak - ing spi - rits bright, What

fun it is to ride and sing a sleigh - ing song to - night!

151

Pat-a-Pan

Burgundian Carol

Merrily

Chil - dren, bring your flute and drum, For the jol - ly time has come; We'll be mer - ry as you play, Tu - ra - lu - ra - lu, pat - a - pat - a - pan, We'll be mer - ry as you play, For a Christ - mas should be gay!

We Wish You a Merry Christmas

With gusto   *Traditional Song*

Now bring us a figgy pudding,
Now bring us a figgy pudding,
Now bring us a figgy pudding,
And bring it out here.

We won't go until we get some,
We won't go until we get some,
We won't go until we get some,
So bring it out here.

We wish you a merry Christmas,
We wish you a merry Christmas,
We wish you a merry Christmas
And a happy New Year!

153

Title Index

Subject Index